MASTERING
PHYSICS

Understanding Quantum Physics

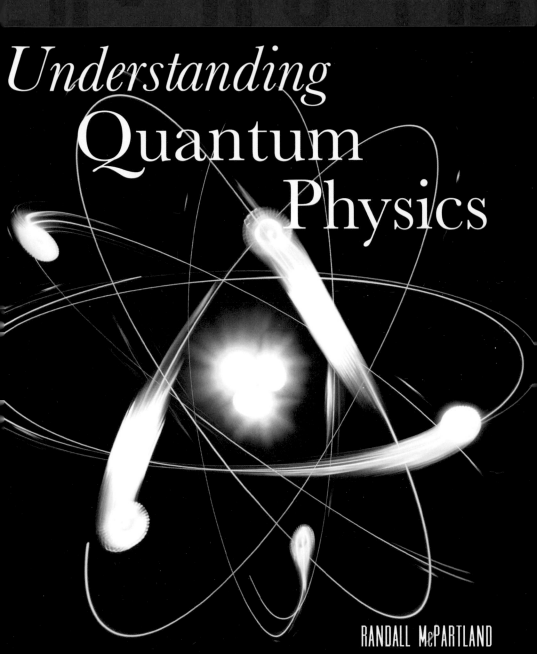

RANDALL McPARTLAND

 Cavendish
Square
New York

Published in 2015 by Cavendish Square Publishing, LLC
243 5th Avenue, Suite 136, New York, NY 10016

Copyright © 2015 by Cavendish Square Publishing, LLC

First Edition

CPSIA Compliance Information: Batch #WW15CSQ

All websites were available and accurate when this book was sent to press.

Library of Congress Cataloging-in-Publication Data

McPartland, Randall.
Understanding quantum physics / by Randall McPartland.
p. cm. — (Mastering physics)
Includes index.
ISBN 978-1-50260-145-2 (hardcover) ISBN 978-1-50260-151-3 (ebook)
1. Spectrum analysis. 2. Photoelectricity. 3. Quantum theory. I. Title.
QC451.M73 2015
530.12—d23

Editor: Fletcher Doyle
Senior Copy Editor: Wendy A. Reynolds
Art Director: Jeffrey Talbot
Senior Designer: Amy Greenan
Senior Production Manager: Jennifer Ryder-Talbot
Production Editor: David McNamara
Photo Research by J8 Media

The photographs in this book are used by permission and through the courtesy of: Cover photo and page 1, Roman Sigaev/iStock/Thinkstock; robertprzybysz/iStock/Thinkstock, 4; Enoch Seeman/The Bridgeman Art Library/Getty Images, 6; File: Thomas Young (scientist).jpg/Wikimedia Commons, 8; ©Universal Images Group Limited/Alamy, 9; Keith Levit Photography/Thinkstock, 10-11; NYPL/Science Source/Photo Researchers/Getty Images, 12; Science Source/Photo Researchers/Getty Images, 13; Dorling Kindersley/Getty Images, 14; Hulton Archive/Getty Images, 16; File:Giordano, Luca Democritus ca 1600.jpg/Wikimedia Commons, 17; Print Collector/Hulton Archive/Getty Images, 18; Encyclopaedia Britannica/ Universal Images Group/Getty Images, 19; Jon Hilmarsson, photographer from Iceland/Moment Open/Getty Images, 20; Look and Learn/Bridgeman Images, 22; Science & Society Picture Library/Getty Images, 25; Designua/Shutterstock.com, 26; File:Bundesarchiv Bild 146-1978-069-26A, Phillipp Lenard.jpg/Wikimedia Commons, 28; BSIP/Science Source, 31; AFP/Getty Images, 33; U.S. Air Force/File:Military laser experiment.jpg/Wikimedia Commons, 35; Universal History Archive/Universal Images Group/Getty Images, 36; Mmaxer/Shutterstock.com, 38; Encyclopaedia Britannica/Universal Images Group/Getty Images, 39; NASA/File:Hubble Space Telescope over Earth (during the STS-109 mission).jpg/Wikimedia Commons, 40; Paul Ehrenfest/File:Niels Bohr Albert Einstein by Ehrenfest.jpg/Wikimedia Commons, 42.

Printed in the United States of America

CONTENTS

INTRODUCTION 4

1 UNDERSTANDING LIGHT 7

2 MODELING THE ATOM 15

3 UNDERSTANDING BLACKBODY RADIATION . . . 21

4 EXPLAINING THE PHOTOELECTRIC EFFECT . . 29

5 EXAMINING LINE SPECTRA 37

GLOSSARY 44

FURTHER INFORMATION 46

BIBLIOGRAPHY 47

INDEX 48

INTRODUCTION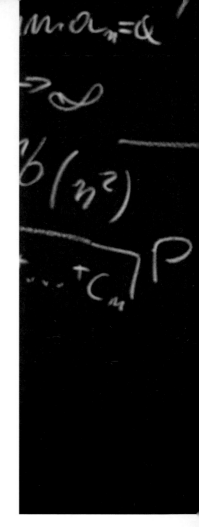

It's a fair statement to say that physics intimidates people. They consider the field to be filled with complicated formulas and daunting information. Some can be convinced of needing to understand the topic when it is tied to real-world applications, such as building machines to make work easier using mechanics, or improving our world through the knowledge of electricity and magnetism. However, convincing someone to learn more about physics becomes even more challenging when the field is **quantum** physics. The study of **subatomic** particles is put on the same plane of difficulty as "brain surgery" and "rocket science" to most. By breaking down the concepts of quantum physics to their simpler building blocks, however, it is possible to grasp and know this challenging branch of physics.

The classical physics of Sir Isaac Newton (1642–1727) lay at the heart of the scientific worldview in the nineteenth century. The first steps into the astonishing new world of quantum physics took place in the early part of the twentieth century. In the span of a few short years, classical physics was overturned, at least for events at the subatomic level.

Those steps had to be taken because classical physics could not explain some of the phenomena scientists were seeing in their experiments. The end result was a whole new way of looking at the subatomic world, and a whole new understanding of the basic structure of the universe. Two of the specific phenomena that could

Learning the building blocks can make it easier to understand quantum physics.

not be understood were the **photoelectric effect** and line spectra, which was a dark or bright line that appeared in an otherwise unbroken spectrum. However, the new branch of physics known as quantum physics could help explain what occurred and why. The value of quantum physics only continues to grow, as scientists use this new view of the microscopic world to better understand a variety of scientific fields, including chemistry, biology, and cosmology. The secrets of subatomic particles will help science better appreciate the larger world and universe.

Sir Isaac Newton developed the laws of physics that hold true until one reaches the subatomic level.

ONE

Understanding Light

S ir Isaac Newton (1642–1727) was one of the most important scientists who ever lived. His laws of gravitation and motion explained how objects move on Earth and in space. He established the science of optics, or the study of the behavior of light, and built the first reflecting telescope. He invented calculus. Among his books are two of the greatest scientific works ever written: *Philosophiae Naturalis Principia Mathematica* (Mathematical Principles of Natural Philosophy), published in 1687, and *Opticks* (Optics), published in 1704.

His work was foundational in helping scientists come to a better understanding of the visible, physical world. Scientists were so sure of their understanding that Pierre-Simon Laplace (1749–1827), a French physicist, claimed at the end of the eighteenth century that if you had unlimited calculating powers and complete knowledge of the position, **mass**, and **velocity** of all particles at any given moment, you could use Newton's equations to predict the future.

However, Newton hadn't solved the nature of light. He had suggested that light might be made up of tiny particles, or what he called "corpuscles." After all, he reasoned, if matter was made up of particles, why shouldn't light be?

Others had different ideas. Christian Huygens (1629–1695) of Holland, who lived at the same time as Newton, thought that perhaps light behaved more like a wave.

Thomas Young shined new light on the wave versus particle theory.

TESTING WAVE THEORY

In 1801, English physicist Thomas Young (1773–1829) came up with an experiment that produced some of the strongest evidence yet that light was wavelike. Young shined light from a single source onto a screen that had two narrow slits in it. The light shone through the slits onto another screen that he had placed a short distance behind the first.

Young reasoned that if light were made up of particles, then each particle should pass straight through one of the slits in the first screen and land on the second screen, creating two bright patches directly behind the slits. If light were wavelike, it would spread out once it had passed through the slits. Waves in the ocean, after all, spread across a harbor after entering it through a gap in the sea wall. If light were a wave, it should pass through the slits, then spread out on the second screen. The light that passed through one slit also would mingle with the light that passed through the other.

When two sets of waves mingle, the results depend on how the waves relate to each other. If they are perfectly in step, then the crests and troughs of one set of waves exactly match the crests

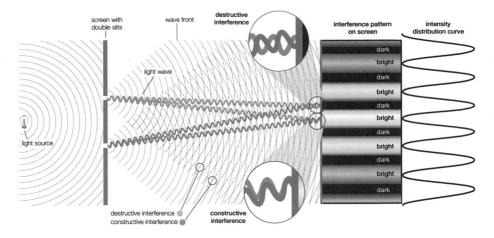

This diagram shows what Thomas Young saw during his famous experiment.

and troughs of the other set of waves, creating extra–high waves. If they are perfectly out of step, then the crests of one set of waves correspond to the troughs of the second set of waves, and the waves cancel each other out, resulting in no apparent waves at all. If they are just slightly out of step, then you get what are called **interference patterns:** sometimes wave crests match up, and sometimes crests match up with troughs. If the waves in question are made of light, this should appear as alternating bands of light and darkness.

When Young shined his light through the two slits in the first screen, this is exactly what he saw on the second screen: alternating light and dark bands. It seemed to be unmistakable evidence that light came in waves, not particles.

LIGHT IN THE ELECTROMAGNETIC SPECTRUM

As the century progressed, it became evident that light, electricity, and magnetism are all linked. Visible light was clearly just a narrow band of frequencies within a much larger **spectrum** of electromagnetic waves. (Different colors of light are simply light waves with different frequencies.) All electromagnetic waves travel

Particles and Waves

To understand why the nature of light mattered, it's important to understand the differences between a particle and a wave. A particle is essentially a discrete object that is usually small in relation to its surroundings. A grain of sand on a beach can be considered a particle; so can a stone in the Great Wall of China. A particle occupies a single, localized volume of space. Its energy is all concentrated within that volume. If you have some means of observing a particle, you can say at any given moment precisely where it is, and how or whether it is moving. A wave is quite different. A wave is a pattern of matter or energy, or both, spread out over a volume of space. Waves are all around us. Waves on a lake or a sea are water waves. A vibrating guitar string is a metal or nylon wave. Sound is an air wave.

There are a number of ways to measure waves. The **wavelength** is the distance between the highest points, or crests, of two successive waves. The **frequency** is how many waves pass a particular point in a certain amount of time. The **amplitude** is how much the wave varies from the normal level of the undisturbed medium: either the height of the crest or the depth of the lowest point, or trough. (In other words, the amplitude of a water wave on a lake is the height of the wave crests above or depths of the wave troughs below the surface level of the water on a perfectly still day.)

Unlike a particle, waves can be spread out over an immense area. A wave doesn't exist in a single location. It's everywhere its crests and troughs are.

The amplitude of an ocean wave is measured from its crest to sea level when the surface is calm.

James Clerk Maxwell showed that all electromagnetic waves travel at the speed of light.

at the same speed, which is the speed of light, just under 300,000 kilometers per second. James Clerk Maxwell (1831–1879) published the equations that spell this out in 1873.

With the realization that light was simply a kind of electromagnetic wave, many physicists thought that all the big

Understanding Quantum Physics

ideas of physics were known. All that was left, it seemed, was a lot of tidying up of the details. In 1894, physicist Albert A. Michelson (1852–1931) said, "The future truths of physical science are to be looked for in the sixth place of decimals."

In fact, as the nineteenth century drew toward its close, a young man in Germany by the name of Max Planck (1858–1947) was warned against going into physics. Physics, he was told, was at the end of its road. There was little worthwhile left to do in the field. Planck fortunately ignored the advice; in a few years he would play a central role in turning classical physics upside down and ushering in the age of quantum physics.

As the nineteenth century ended, physicists decided to turn their attention from the nature of light to a new problem, the construction of the **atom**. Although they originally thought they understood how the pieces of the atom fit together, scientists decided to take a deeper look at the concept.

Max Planck turned classical physics upside down.

The currant bun model of the atom was proposed by John Thomson.

TWO

Modeling the Atom

B ritish physicist Joseph John Thomson (1856–1940) was the first person to prove that the atom, the existence of which was first theorized in the fifth century BCE, was not the smallest division of matter.

In 1897, Thomson fused two metal terminals into the ends of a glass tube out of which most of the air had been removed, then passed an electrical current between the terminals. With a strong enough **vacuum** in the tube, a bright green glow appeared next to the positive terminal. When Thomson placed a magnet next to the positive terminal, he could make the green glow move.

That glow, and the magnet's effect on it, indicated to Thomson that electricity was actually the movement of tiny discrete particles, each with a negative electrical charge. Thomson was able to show that each of these particles, eventually called **electrons**, had a mass of around 9.11×10^{-31} kilograms. That's about 1/1800 of the mass of the smallest known atom, that of hydrogen.

Thomson noticed that the mass of the electron was the same no matter what material was used in the **cathode**, or negative terminal,

John Thomson theorized that negatively charged electrons orbited around a sphere of positive electricity.

out of which the electrons came. That indicated to him that all atoms, regardless of their element, must contain electrons. Atoms, therefore, were no longer the smallest possible particle.

The next year, John Thomson suggested the atom might consist of negatively charged electrons distributed around a kind of diffuse sphere of positive electricity. This became known as the "currant bun" or "plum pudding" model of the atom—the electrons were the currants or plums, and the positive charge was the bun or the pudding.

The currant bun model of the atom didn't hold up long. Scientists studying radioactivity had realized that it consisted of streams of particles, just as electricity did. Ernest Rutherford (1871–1937), who had studied with Thomson, and his assistant, Frederick Soddy (1877–1956), identified three types of radioactivity: alpha rays, beta rays, and gamma rays. Moreover, Rutherford had suggested that radioactivity from substances such as uranium or radium was the result of atoms of the substances spontaneously transforming into atoms of a different kind, releasing radioactive particles in the process.

Understanding Quantum Physics

The theories of Greek philosopher Democritus were not improved upon for more than two thousand years.

Forward Thinking

The ancient Greeks didn't have high-powered microscopes to see matter at the atomic level, so they used another tool at which they excelled: philosophy.

In about the year 400 BCE, the philosopher Democritus asked what would happen if you took a piece of matter and broke it in half until it could be divided no more. He called this last piece the atom, which is by definition something that is indivisible. Democritus said that all matter was made up of tiny particles, and that the different properties of matter were the result of interactions between these small particles.

His ideas were not improved upon for centuries. In 1808, chemist John Dalton published his atomic theories. He stated that all matter is made up of atoms that are indivisible and indestructible, that all atoms of a specific element are the same in mass and properties, and that compounds are formed by two or more types of atoms.

The naming of the electron, the light particle that carries the electric charge, came in the late nineteenth century. Electron comes from the Greek word for amber. In 600 BCE, Thales of Miletus was the first person to observe **static electricity** when he noticed that amber rubbed with fur would attract bits of feather and hair. However, he incorrectly attributed the attracting force to the amber and not to an atomic particle.

This transformation of atoms from one kind to another, together with the release of particles, provided another indication that the atom was not indestructible. Rutherford produced the first artificially induced nuclear reaction in 1919, inspiring much of the later work that led to nuclear power and nuclear weapons. The rutherford, a unit of radioactivity, is named in his honor.

A unit of radiation is named for Ernest Rutherford.

Rutherford and Soddy's new understanding of radioactivity also provided a different way to study the inside of atoms and to see if they really did look like currant buns. By firing a stream of particles at a target (Rutherford used a thin gold film) and then studying how the target's atoms deflected that stream of particles, you could make an educated guess about the structure of those atoms.

The results were much different than expected. If atoms were like currant buns, then the massive alpha particles should have gone right through them, deflected only slightly. Instead, although most of the alpha rays went right through the gold film, some were deflected quite a bit. Even more unexpectedly, some of the alpha rays actually bounced back. Rutherford said later that it was as astonishing as if a naval shell had bounced off a sheet of tissue paper.

Rutherford realized that the currant bun model of the atom could not be correct. The only way the gold atoms could substantially deflect the alpha rays was if the positive charge in the gold atoms was concentrated at the center of the atom instead of being spread out.

The currant bun model of the atom gave way to the solar system model. Just like the solar system consists mostly of empty space, with most of its mass concentrated in the central Sun, around which the much-less-massive planets orbit, so the atom was thought

Understanding Quantum Physics

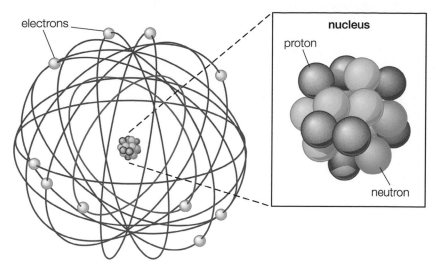

Ernest Rutherford's model of a neon atom had the look of the solar system.

to be mostly empty space, with most of its mass concentrated in a tiny, positively charged central **nucleus**, orbited by the much-less-massive (and even tinier) negatively charged electrons.

LIMITATIONS OF THE PLANETARY MODEL

The new solar system model of the atom solved some problems, but it also posed new ones. Electrons orbiting the nucleus of an atom must be constantly changing direction. Everything that was known about electromagnetic theory then stated that whenever an electron changed direction, it should radiate away some of its energy. That loss of energy would slow the electrons, so that they should be pulled closer and closer to the nucleus. The only possible outcome would be the collapse of the atom. Because atoms are so small, this collapse should occur very quickly—in less than a millionth of a second.

If atoms did collapse, no matter would exist in the universe, and because the universe does exist, there had to be a way to explain the behavior of the electrons. A new branch of physics known as quantum physics provided the explanation, and it would counter what physicists thought they knew about the subatomic world.

Modeling the Atom

The Aurora Borealis is created when charged particles from the sun enter the Earth's atmosphere above the North Pole and collide with gas particles. The green color indicates low altitude oxygen, the purple indicates nitrogen, and the red, high altitude oxygen.

THREE

Understanding Blackbody Radiation

Physicists in the late eighteenth and early nineteenth centuries began to reexamine some of the conclusions that they had drawn about both the construction of the atom, as well as the fundamental nature of electromagnetic **radiation**. In the nineteenth century, a branch of physics called statistical physics would study the properties of complicated systems. If one had a large volume of a specific gas, that volume would have a large number of atoms, and scientists could not predict the behavior of all those individual atoms. However, they could predict the behavior of the entire volume of gas. Each atom may be impossible to predict, but the actions of the group of atoms as a whole can be guessed through mathematical modeling. While this approach worked on many complicated systems, physicists began to notice some exceptions.

PREDICTING BLACKBODY RADIATION

In 1900, English physicist Lord Rayleigh (1842–1919) attempted to apply statistical physics to another complex system, the distribution of different frequencies in **blackbody** radiation, and discovered

Lord Rayleigh developed an experiment that showed flaws in our understanding of electromagnetic waves.

that classical physics could not accurately predict the distribution of those frequencies.

A blackbody is a hypothetical object that first perfectly absorbs all the radiation on its surface, then perfectly re-emits it all. Although there's no way to build a true blackbody, physicists could approximate one using a special oven. Essentially, this oven was an empty box containing electromagnetic energy.

In such an oven, there had to be some sort of equilibrium. If more energy existed in the walls than in the interior, energy would move from the walls to the interior. If more energy existed in the interior than in the walls, energy would move from the interior to the walls. That meant that both the walls and the interior of the box should have a comparable amount of energy, and should be the same temperature.

It was easy enough to build the special oven and to look inside it to measure the frequencies of the electromagnetic waves inside it. Scientists knew those frequencies would be limited by the size of the box. In other words, the waves had to fit inside the box. The lowest possible frequency would be one at which the wavelength exactly fit inside the box. After that, you could have twice the lowest frequency (called the second harmonic), then three times the lowest frequency (the third harmonic), and so on to infinity (the millionth, billionth, trillionth harmonic—and beyond).

According to what was understood about electromagnetic waves at the end of the nineteenth century, each wave carried an energy that was proportional to its frequency and to its amplitude. Even the millionth billionth trillionth harmonic would carry some share of the overall energy of the wave. However, if you could have an infinite number of harmonics, and each carried some energy, then the total amount of energy carried by the wave was also infinite—and most of the energy would be carried by extremely high frequencies. If you built a special oven to approximate blackbody radiation, then, according to classical physics, that box would contain an infinite amount of energy. When physicists built such ovens and looked inside to see how much electromagnetic energy they contained and at what frequencies, however, the ovens clearly did not contain an infinite amount of energy. If they had, we'd be using them as power sources.

These extremely high frequencies of electromagnetic radiation, higher than those of visible light, are collectively called ultraviolet, because they lie "ultra," which is Latin for "beyond," the violet end of the visible spectrum. As a result, the inability to accurately predict the distribution of different frequencies in blackbody radiation became known as the "ultraviolet catastrophe." It was called a catastrophe because it represented a huge failure of classical physics.

There seemed to be no way in which classical physics could be modified to predict what was really seen in blackbody radiation experiments. You couldn't divide the observed amount of energy

Planck's Triumph and Tragedy

Max Planck was a professor of physics at the University of Berlin from 1889 until 1928, and his development of quantum theory earned him the 1918 Nobel Prize in Physics.

Sometimes scientists who make great discoveries don't realize what they've done. That wasn't the case with Planck; he told his son that he believed he had made a discovery as significant as those of Newton. It may have sounded like bragging at the time, but he was exactly right.

However, his successes were tempered by difficulties. He was married twice. His first wife, Marie Merck, died in 1909. Planck then married her cousin, Marga. He had five children, but three of them died young, leaving him with two sons.

In 1930, Planck was elected president of the Kaiser Wilhelm Society for the Advancement of Science. In the 1930s, he criticized the Nazi regime, particularly over its treatment of Jews, and was forced out of the society.

He suffered two losses during World War II (1939–1945). One son was executed in 1944 for a failed plot to assassinate Adolph Hitler. Allied bombs then destroyed his house in the war's late stages.

He became president of the society again after the war. He died in 1947, and the society was renamed the Max Planck Society.

Max Planck was removed as head of a society for the advancement of science because of his criticism of the Nazis in his homeland.

THE ELECTROMAGNETIC SPECTRUM

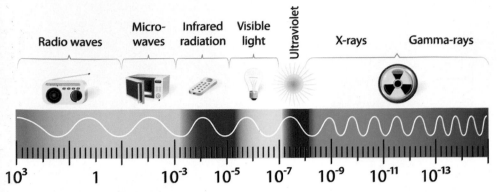

This vector diagram shows different types of electromagnetic radiation by their wavelengths, from lower to higher frequencies.

among the infinite number of harmonics, because then you would end up with an infinitely small amount of energy, essentially nothing, being carried by each frequency. Nor could you give each of the infinite number of possible frequencies a little bit of energy, because then you would end up with infinite energy inside the box. What you really got inside the box was a progression of frequencies similar to those that blacksmiths saw every time they heated up metal for working. As the temperature increased, the inside of the box began to glow in different colors, first orange-red, then a brighter yellow, and finally a hot blue-white.

SOLVING THE ULTRAVIOLET CATASTROPHE

In 1900, the same year Rayleigh discovered the ultraviolet catastrophe, Max Planck (1858–1947), a professor of physics at the University of Berlin from 1889 to 1928, explained it away.

Planck's proposal avoided the ultraviolet catastrophe by making the energy content of the electromagnetic waves inside the special blackbody oven finite instead of potentially infinite. The very high-frequency waves, the trillionth harmonic, and so on, never arose, because the minimum amount of energy required for them to exist exceeded the total amount of energy in the box.

Understanding Quantum Physics

In classical physics, physicists thought that radiation oozed in and out of a blackbody (or in and out of the walls of the special oven). Planck suggested radiation might instead be emitted or absorbed in packets of energy of a definite size. He called these packets of energy quanta.

His word choice provided the name for a new physics known as quantum physics. Quantum physics would dominate the twentieth century as classical physics had dominated the nineteenth.

EXPANDING QUANTUM THEORY

What gave rise to the ultraviolet catastrophe was the need for each electromagnetic wave, no matter how tiny its wavelength, to carry some portion of the overall energy. Planck suggested instead that there must be some absolute minimum amount of energy, proportional to the wave's frequency, carried by each quantum. The energy carried by an electromagnetic wave would therefore have to be a multiple of that minimum. To be more precise, it would be a whole number times the wave's frequency, multiplied by a conversion factor that Planck calculated and that has become known as Planck's constant. It's approximately 6.6×10^{-34} joule-seconds, and is represented by the symbol h.

Mathematically, Planck said that an individual atom vibrating at a particular frequency (represented by the Greek letter n) could emit energy only in multiples of hn. It could emit energy of $1hn$, $2hn$, $3hn$, etc., but nothing less than hn, and no fractional multiples of hn.

However, the importance of Planck's discovery wasn't immediately apparent. At first, scientists weren't sure what to make of Planck's idea. While it avoided the ultraviolet catastrophe, they weren't certain if it had any other practical use.

FOUR

Explaining the Photoelectric Effect

In the early twentieth century, scientists were looking to explain a problem that did not have an explanation when examined through the lens of classical physics. It was known as the photoelectric effect. Scientists could create conditions where metals would emit electrons when light was shined upon them. Scientists assumed that the energy from the light was transferred to the electrons of the metal, which would cause the electrons to increase their speed to the point where they could break away from their atoms. However, the behavior of these electrons did not match what classical physics would have predicted.

The number of electrons released could be determined by measuring the electrical current flowing through a wire connected to the metal. The amount of **kinetic energy** the electrons carried could be measured by the force (in the form of an electrical charge applied to the metal) that was needed to stop them from moving.

Philipp Lenard discovered the importance of wave frequency to kinetic energy in the photoelectric effect.

EXPERIMENTS TO EXPLAIN THE PHOTOELECTRIC EFFECT

In 1902, a German physicist named Philipp Lenard (1862–1947) discovered various important properties of the photoelectric effect. First, he discovered that the greater the intensity of the incoming light, the greater the number of electrons that were released. That observation made sense. After all, when bigger, more powerful waves start hitting an ocean beach, they dislodge more sand than smaller, weaker waves.

However, Lenard's next discovery did not make sense in the world of classical physics. He discovered that the kinetic energy contained in each of the escaping electrons did not increase when the intensity of the light increased. In beach terms, more sand was being dislodged, but no more violently by the more powerful waves than sand was by the weaker waves. In other words, even though the light wave was carrying more energy, none of that energy was being used to speed up the electrons. According to the laws of thermodynamics, energy couldn't be created or destroyed. Where was that extra energy going?

Lenard then discovered that while increasing the intensity of the light didn't increase the kinetic energy of the escaping electrons, increasing the frequency of the light did. It was as if little, fast-moving waves were able to dislodge sand from a beach more violently than slower-moving giant waves, which isn't what happens. In fact, below a certain frequency, no electrons were dislodged from the metal no matter how intense the light was. Contrarily, electrons above a certain frequency were dislodged from the metal no matter how weak the light was.

Different metals required different frequencies of light to exhibit the photoelectric effect. Green light, or low-frequency light, could expel electrons from sodium metal. To produce electrons from copper or aluminum, however, you needed high-frequency ultraviolet light.

Lenard's investigation of the photoelectric effect produced this basic equation:

$$\tfrac{1}{2}mv^2 = hn - K$$

In this equation, *m* is the mass of an escaping electron, *v* is its velocity, $\frac{1}{2}mv^2$ is the standard formula used to calculate kinetic energy, *n* is the frequency of the light wave, *h* is Planck's constant (6.6×10^{-34} joule-seconds), and *K* is a number that varies from metal to metal.

Higher intensity light waves of a sufficient frequency (blue) will increase the number of electrons produced by the photoelectric effect, but low-frequency waves (red) will produce no electrons regardless of intensity.

QUANTA AND THE PHOTOELECTRIC EFFECT

No one starting from the assumption that light is a wave could make sense of Lenard's findings. Albert Einstein's breakthrough was to realize that Planck's idea of energy packets, or quanta, could be used to explain the photoelectric effect.

If light consisted of a stream of quanta instead of being a continuous wave, then an electron would be ejected from the metal because one of these quanta had hit it. In the process, the quanta would transfer all its energy to the electron.

In Planck's theory, the amount of energy in each quantum of light was directly proportional to the frequency of the light. This hypothesis meant that if the frequency were too low, the quantum of light would not be carrying enough energy to dislodge any electron. That explained why no electrons were produced below a certain critical frequency, differing from metal to metal, no matter how intense the light beam might be.

Raising the frequency would increase the energy carried by each quantum. Once the frequency was high enough for the

Providing Building Blocks

The strength of science is the foundational nature of what is discovered, and how the next generation of scientists uses that foundation to further their field. Planck's quanta would inspire a young scientist working in a patent office in Switzerland to solve another problem that seemed to have no explanation when using classical physics. This application of quanta would help the scientific world understand the importance of quantum physics in understanding the nature of the universe. This young patent clerk was Albert Einstein.

Einstein entered the Swiss Federal Polytechnic School in 1896, with the goal of becoming a teacher of physics and mathematics. He became a citizen of Switzerland when he graduated in 1901, but was not able to find a teaching position. He took a position as a technical assistant in the patent office.

While working at the patent office and studying for his doctorate, which he received in 1905, he did some of his most remarkable work. Included was his research on the photoelectric effect, for which he was awarded the Nobel Prize in Physics in 1921. (He did not receive one for his theory of relativity, as most people suppose).

Einstein became a German citizen in 1914, but renounced it in 1933 for political reasons. He moved to the United States to take a position as a professor of theoretical physics at Princeton. He considered his achievements as stepping-stones for the next discovery.

Albert Einstein earned his Nobel Prize while studying for his doctorate.

quanta to carry enough energy to dislodge electrons, increasing the frequency would also increase the energy imparted to the electrons. That increase in energy would impart a higher velocity to the dislodged electrons.

In Einstein's theory, increasing the intensity of the light beam would simply increase the number of quanta present in the light beam. The increase in quanta would increase the overall number of electrons produced by making it more likely that quanta of light would collide with electrons. However, the increase in quanta would have no effect on the velocity of the ejected electrons.

CREATING AN EQUATION FOR PHOTONS

These quanta of light became known as **photons**. In Einstein's theory of light, the energy carried by each photon is entirely determined by the frequency, expressed by:

$$E = hn$$

where E is energy, h is Planck's constant, and n is the frequency of the light.

The reason we don't ordinarily notice that light is made up of individual photons instead of smooth, continuous waves, is that the amount of energy carried by individual photons is extremely tiny.

Experiments by American physicist Robert A. Millikan (1868–1953) in 1915 verified Einstein's theory.

REDEFINING LIGHT

Einstein's breakthrough on the photoelectric effect didn't just solve one problem, it reopened a debate long considered settled. For years scientists had tried to discover whether light was made up of particles or waves. The previous century's experiments had concluded that light's behavior was consistent with waves. However, Einstein's explanation of the photoelectric effect seemed to define light as a particle. Could light somehow be both? Physicists did not think this was possible, but theories and experiments by one side

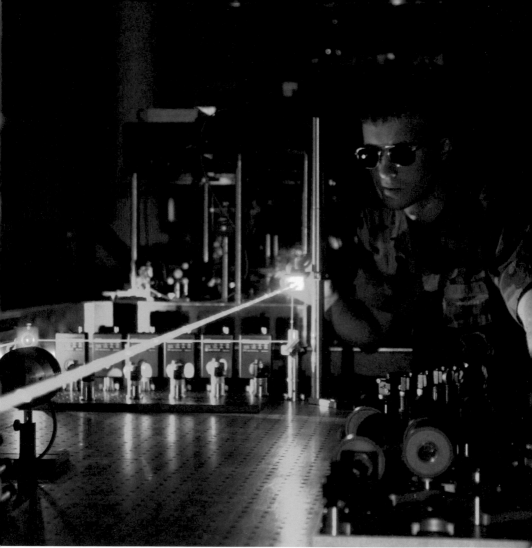

Experiments on the photoelectric effect are now being done with high intensity lasers.

(Young and Maxwell) supported "light as a wave" and the other side (Einstein and Planck) supported "light as quanta, or particles." Solving this contradiction would become a matter of great importance to twentieth-century physicists.

A continuous spectrum with Fraunhofer lines is juxtaposed with other spectra.

1. Continuous Spectrum with Fraunhofer's lines ; 2, Spectrum of Sodium ; 3, Do. of Potassium ; 4, Do. of Stron
5, Absorption Spectrum of Arterial blood, diluted 1 in 250 ; 6, Do. diluted 1 in 400 ; 7, Same as No. 6 but de
of Oxygen ; 8, Absorption Spectrum of Chlorophyll in Alcohol.

FIVE

Examining Line Spectra

I t was Sir Isaac Newton who discovered that traditional white light could be broken into colored bands through the use of a glass prism. These bands would follow the colors of the rainbow, and Newton named this the "spectrum." In 1814, German physicist Joseph von Fraunhofer (1787–1826) discovered that if the Sun's spectrum was spread widely enough, it was crossed by a large number of fine dark lines. These lines are now known as Fraunhofer lines.

To create his spectra, Fraunhofer pioneered the use of the diffraction grating, which is an array of very fine slits in an opaque screen, or a screen of fine wires very close together. Light passing through the slits or between the wires produces interference patterns, but these patterns show the colors of the spectrum. Diffraction grating of various types continues to be used in spectroscopy today.

As the nineteenth century progressed, scientists studied the spectra produced by light sources such as flames, electrical arcs, and sparks. Within the spectra of these light sources were bright lines. Then, in 1848, the French physicist Jean-Bernard-Leon Foucault

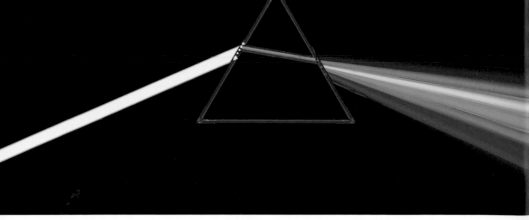

Light shown through a prism is separated into its component colors.

(1819–1868) discovered that a flame containing sodium would absorb yellow light coming from a strong electrical arc placed behind it.

STUDYING THE HYDROGEN SPECTRUM

In 1885, a Swiss schoolmaster named Johann Jakob Balmer (1825–1898), by carefully studying the hydrogen spectrum, came up with a simple, accurate formula

$$\frac{1}{\lambda} = R\left(\frac{1}{2^2} - \frac{1}{n^2}\right)$$

where λ is the wavelength at which the visible lines in the spectrum of hydrogen appear, R is a constant, and n is simply an integer that described the wavelengths of hydrogen's four visible spectral lines. In a way, this was the first hint of quantum physics, though no one recognized it. Experimentation by other scientists showed that Balmer's equation also predicted the location of other spectral lines in the hydrogen spectrum outside of the range of visible light. The explanation for the Balmer equation came almost thirty years after it was formulated, from a young Danish scientist named Niels Bohr.

Understanding Quantum Physics

By 1912, Bohr was considering various problems with the new planetary model of the atom, including its inability to explain line spectra. He was familiar with Planck's finding that energy could come in discrete packets, or quanta, instead of continuous waves. He also knew about Einstein's photons, another example of quanta.

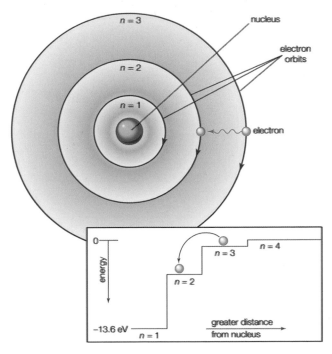

Niels Bohr explained the different orbits of electrons.

In 1913, Bohr suggested extending these new quantum ideas to the atom. Bohr suggested, first, that for some reason as yet unknown, the electrons orbiting the nucleus of an atom did not radiate energy, even though Maxwell's equations governing electromagnetic radiation said they should. (Remember that if they did radiate energy, they would quickly lose enough energy to collapse into the nucleus, and the universe as we know it couldn't exist.) Instead, Bohr suggested, electrons can move around the nucleus of an atom in stable orbits with no loss of energy, but not in any conceivable orbit. Bohr said electrons were limited to a very few specific orbits.

Examining Line Spectra

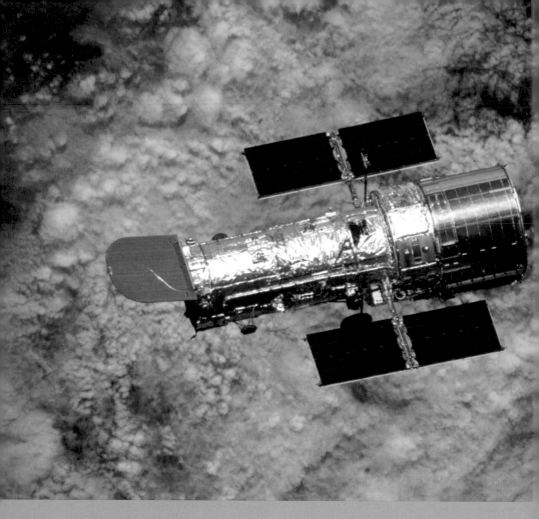

Spectrum Patterns of Elements

The Hubble Space Telescope observes light frequencies that can't penetrate Earth's atmosphere.

In 1859, Gustav Kirchhoff (1824–1887) showed that each element, when heated until it was incandescent, produced a characteristic pattern of bright lines. This pattern meant you could determine the chemical makeup of a light source by studying its spectrum. (Fellow German Robert Bunsen, inventor of the Bunsen burner, aided Kirchhoff in this discovery.) Kirchhoff also concluded that the dark lines Fraunhofer had seen were the result of elements at the surface of the Sun absorbing part of the continuous spectrum of light emitted from the much hotter interior. Since Fraunhofer lines indicated which elements were present at the Sun's surface, you could use them to analyze the atmosphere of the Sun.

Similarly, you could use spectroscopy to analyze the chemical makeup of distant stars. Astronomers quickly set about to conduct such analyses, even though no one had a good explanation for why there should be distinct spectral lines for each element. According to classical physics, there was no reason why a heated element shouldn't produce a continuous spectrum. One spectrum that was frequently observed was the spectrum of hydrogen, because it is the most abundant element in the universe.

Not all wavelengths can get through Earth's atmosphere so some observations must be made from telescopes located in satellites. The Hubble Space Telescope is the most well known of these.

Niels Bohr and Albert Einstein relax at the home of physicist Paul Ehrenfest on December 11, 1925.

Understanding Quantum Physics

The reason, he said, was that the amount of angular momentum, or spin, that the electrons could have as they circled the nucleus had to be a whole-number multiple of some basic unit. In classical physics terms, none of this explanation made any sense. If the atom were really structured like the solar system, then a vast number of orbits should have been possible, and so should any amount of spin.

ELECTRON COLLISIONS

Bohr pointed out that for an electron to jump from one stable orbit to another—to increase or decrease its spin—it had to either gain or lose energy. If an electron loses spin and drops to a lower orbit, he said, it ejects energy in the form of a photon.

The usual way for an electron to gain energy would be via a collision with another particle. Collisions became more likely when substances were heated, because the atoms in the substance would then vibrate more rapidly. Occasionally such a collision would give an electron some extra energy, enough to make it jump to a higher orbit. After a while, it would slip back down to its regular orbit, and in doing so, it would eject a photon.

Once an electron had reached its lowest possible orbit, no more energy could be lost. Unlike Rutherford's original planetary model of the atom, Bohr's model could explain why atoms don't collapse.

Bohr was able to calculate what the frequency of the radiation ejected by an electron jumping from a higher stable orbit to a lower one should be in heated hydrogen. That frequency matched up precisely with the Balmer formula. The sharp spectral lines seen from heated hydrogen were the result of photons of specific frequencies being ejected from electrons as they dropped from a higher to a lower stable orbit.

So now Planck's quanta had a second application that revolutionized physics. Just as Einstein had used the quanta theory to better explain light, Bohr was able to use quanta to create a better atomic model. This new model fundamentally changed how science understood the basic nature of how the world works.

GLOSSARY

amplitude The maximum extent of a vibration or oscillation, measured from the position of equilibrium.

atom The smallest possible unit of an element, consisting of a nucleus orbited by electrons.

blackbody A hypothetical object that perfectly absorbs all the radiation on its surface, then perfectly reemits it all.

cathode The electron-emitting or negative electrode of an electron tube.

electrons Negatively charged particles that are one of the basic components of the atom.

frequency The number of wave crests (or troughs) that pass a given point in a given amount of time.

interference patterns An overall pattern created when two or more waves interfere with each other.

kinetic energy The energy that a body possesses by being in motion.

mass A measure of the amount of matter in an object.

nucleus The central part of an atom, around which electrons orbit.

photoelectric effect The release of electrons caused by light shining on metal.

photon A particle representing a quantum of light or other electromagnetic radiation.

quantum (plural, quanta) A tiny, discrete packet of energy.

radiation The emission of energy in the form of particles or waves.

spectrum The series of colors produced by shining a beam of light through a prism or diffraction grating.

static electricity A charge created when electrons are transferred from one object to another.

subatomic Having to do with particles smaller than the atom.

vacuum A space absolutely devoid of matter.

velocity The speed at which an object is moving in a particular direction.

wavelength The distance between one wave crest (or trough) and the next.

FURTHER INFORMATION

BOOKS

Ford, Kenneth W. *The Quantum World: Quantum Physics for Everyone.* Cambridge, MA: Harvard University Press, 2014.

Gao, Shan. *Quantum Mechanics: A Comprehensible Introduction for Students.* New York, NY: Amazon Kindle Direct Publishing, 2014.

McEvoy, J. P. *Introducing Quantum Theory: A Graphic Guide.* Cambridge, England: Icon Books Ltd., 2014.

Susskind, Leonard, and Art Friedman. *Quantum Physics: The Theoretical Minimum.* New York, NY: Basic Books, 2014.

WEBSITES

Quantum Physics for Dummies Cheat Sheet
www.dummies.com/how-to/content/quantum-physics-for-dummies-cheat-sheet.html

Serving as a companion to the book *Quantum Physics for Dummies*, this site explains some of the basic concepts of the field and provides associated formulas.

Science Daily's Page Devoted to Quantum Physics News
www.sciencedaily.com/news/matter_energy/quantum_physics

This site provides an excellent collection of articles about the latest breakthroughs in quantum physics.

Understanding Quantum Mechanics and its Implications
implications-of-quantum-physics.com/index.html

This site explains quantum physics by breaking down the topic in detail.

BIBLIOGRAPHY

Blood, Casey. "Understanding Quantum Mechanics and Its Implications." http://implications-of-quantum-physics.com/index.html

Kuhn, Karl F. *Basic Physics: A Self-Teaching Guide.* 2nd ed. New York: John Wiley & Sons, Inc., 1996.

Lindley, David. *Where Does the Weirdness Go?* New York: Basic Books, 1996.

McEvoy, J. P. *Introducing Quantum Theory: A Graphic Guide.* Cambridge, England: Icon Books Ltd., 2014.

Polkinghorne, John. *Quantum Theory: A Very Short Introduction.* New York: Oxford University Press, 2002.

Rae, Alistair. *Quantum Physics: A Beginner's Guide.* London, England: Oneworld Publications, 2011.

Susskind, Leonard, and Art Friedman. *Quantum Physics: The Theoretical Minimum.* New York: Basic Books, 2014.

INDEX

Page numbers in **boldface** are illustrations.

amplitude, 10, **10**, 23
atom, **14**, 15–19, **19**, 27, 29, 43
    collapse of, 19, 43
    construction of, 13, 21
    planetary model of, 39, 43
    transformation of, 18
    See also, currant bun

blackbody, 21–23, 26–27

cathode, 15
currant bun, **14**, 16, 18

electrons, 15–17, **16**, 19, 29–31, **31**, 34, 39, 43

frequency, 26–27, **29**, **31**, 34
    definition of, 10
    harmonics, 23, 26
    of light, 30–31, 34
    of radiation, 43

interference patterns, 9, 37

kinetic energy, 29–31, **29**

mass, 7, 17–19, 31
    of the electron, 15

nucleus, 19, 43
    electrons orbiting, 19, 39

photoelectric effect, 5, 29–32, **29**, **31**, 34–35
photon, 34, 43
    Einstein's photons, 39
    equation, 34

quantum, 4–5, **5–6**, 13, 19, 24, 32, 38–39
    light, 31
    theory, 27

radiation, **18**, 21–22, 27, 43
    electromagnetic radiation, 23, **26**, 39
    See also, blackbody
rays
    alpha ray, 16, 18
    beta ray, 16
    gamma ray, 16

spectrum, 5, 9, 23, **36**, 37–38, 41
static electricity, 17
subatomic, 4–5, **6**, 19

vacuum, 15
velocity, 7, 31, 34

wavelength, 10, 23, **26**, 27, 38, 41

Understanding Quantum Physics